D0890200

JOHNSTON MIDDLE SCHOOL LIBRARY
10410 MANHATTAN DR.
HOUSTON, TEXAS 77096-5299

THE INDIAN WARS

WITHDRAWN

THE INDIAN WARS

Rebecca Stefoff

JOHNSTON MIDDLE SCHOOL LIBRARY
10410 MANHATTAN DR.
HOUSTON, TEXAS 77096-5299

BENCHMARK BOOKS

MARSHALL CAVENDISH
NEW YORK

Benchmark Books
Marshall Cavendish
99 White Plains Road
Tarrytown, New York 10591

Copyright © 2003 Rebecca Stefoff

All rights reserved. No part of this book may be reproduced or utilized in any form
or by any means electronic or mechanical including photocopying, recording, or by any information
storage and retrieval system, without permission from the copyright holders.

• • •

Library of Congress Cataloging-in-Publication Data
Stefoff, Rebecca, 1951–
The Indian wars/by Rebecca Stefoff
p. cm—(North American historical atlases)
Includes bibliographical references and index.
Summary: Conflicts with colonists: Jamestown and the Powhatan Tribes, The Pequot War, King Philip's War,
the Pueblo Revolt, the French and Indian War—The wars of removal: Beyond the mountains, Tecumseh's dream,
the Indian Removal Act, the Seminole Wars—Fighting for the West: Bloodshed in the Pacific Northwest,
the Navajo and Apache Wars, the fate of the Plains Indians, the end of resistance.
ISBN 0-7614-1348-0 (lib.bdg.)
1. Indians of North America—Wars—Juvenile literature.   [1. Indians of North America—Wars.]   I. Title.
E81 .S74   2003   2002006192   973—dc21

• • •

Printed in Hong Kong
1 3 5 7 8 6 4 2

• • •

Book Designer: Judith Turziano
Photo Researcher: Candlepants Incorporated

• • •

CREDITS
Front Cover: Mapp of New England by John Seller, 1675, Library of Congress, Map Division, Washington, D.C.
Back Cover: *Corbis*

The photographs in this book are used by permission and through the courtesy of:
Bridgeman Art Library/ Private Collection: 2–3, 7, 8; *Corbis:* Bettmann, 11, 13, 19 left & right, 24, 40; *Corbis:* 21, 26, 39;
Smithsonian American Art Museum, Washington D.C./Art Resource, NY: 30, 33; *Denver Public Library/Western History Department:* 37

Contents

Chapter One

CONFLICTS

WITH

COLONISTS

The Indian wars began almost as soon as the first European **colonists** arrived in North America. An estimated 4.5 million Native Americans lived in North America when Christopher Columbus landed in the Americas in 1492. Thinking he had reached India, Columbus called them *Indians.* His mistake didn't keep other Europeans from following him to the Americas. They came as conquerors, **missionaries**, and colonists. Soon the trickle of newcomers swelled into a mighty wave that swept the Indians from their homes—and nearly swept them out of existence. At first, Native Americans and Europeans often came together peacefully, but as time went on there were more and more violent confrontations. The Indians fought for four hundred years to hold on to their land.

Jamestown and the Powhatan Tribes

The English founded Jamestown in 1607 on Virginia's James River. It was the first lasting North American **colony**. A chieftain of the Powhatan tribe governed a confederacy of thirty-two tribes there. The English called both the people and their leader Powhatan.

Many colonists died of hunger and sickness in Jamestown's early years. More would have perished without the corn and meat they got from Powhatan's people in exchange for tools, cloth, and other goods. Legend says that

An English illustration from the seventeenth century shows colonists landing at Jamestown. Native Americans crouch at their feet or stand in the shadows. From the start, most colonists viewed the Indians as lesser beings whose proper purpose was to aid the settlers.

Captain John Smith, a founder and leader of the colony, won the friendship of Powhatan's daughter Pocahontas, who later married another colonist. In spite of such connections, colonists and Indians sometimes came into

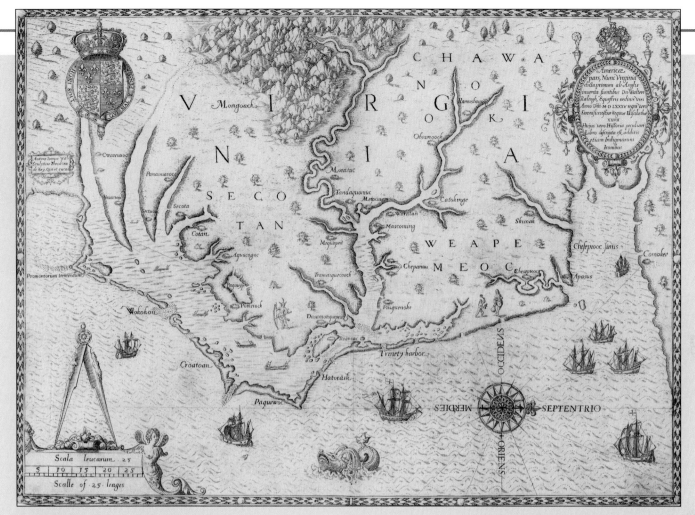

Published in 1580, this map of the Virginia coast was drawn by John White, who had gone to Virginia five years earlier. (In the style of mapmaking White used, north is to the right.) The map shows European ships sailing toward the coast. The smaller vessels are Native American canoes, and the figure with a bow and arrow on the shore represents the Indians of the region. White made many drawings of the landscapes, animals, and people of North America. These pictures gave most Europeans their first glimpse of the "New World" across the Atlantic Ocean.

conflict. The colony kept growing, and so did the colonists' demands. The people of Jamestown took what they wanted—the Indians' fields and food—and did not always pay for it.

Chief Powhatan died in 1618. Four years later, Opechancanough, Powhatan's brother

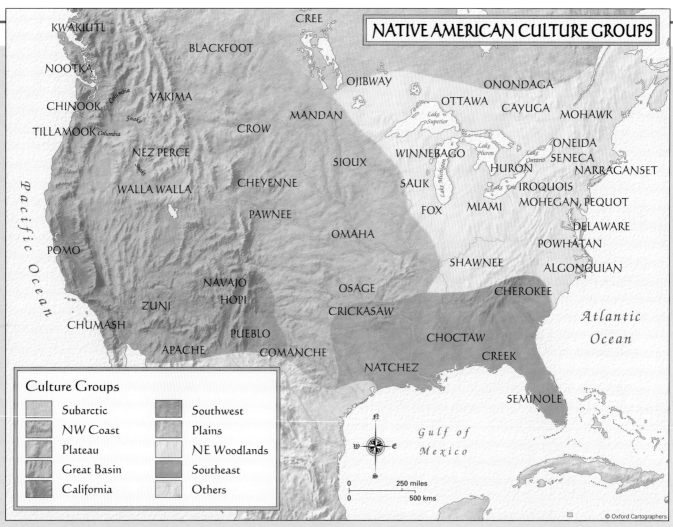

NATIVE AMERICAN CULTURE GROUPS

KWAKIUTL
CREE
BLACKFOOT
NOOTKA
OJIBWAY
ONONDAGA
OTTAWA
CAYUGA
YAKIMA
CHINOOK
Columbia
MANDAN
MOHAWK
Snake
CROW
ONEIDA
TILLAMOOK Columbia
SENECA
NEZ PERCE
WINNEBAGO
HURON
NARRAGANSET
SIOUX
Snake
WALLA WALLA
CHEYENNE
SAUK
IROQUOIS
MIAMI
MOHEGAN, PEQUOT
PAWNEE
FOX
Pacific Ocean
OMAHA
DELAWARE
POWHATAN
POMO
SHAWNEE
ALGONQUIAN
NAVAJO
OSAGE
CHEROKEE
ZUNI
HOPI
CRICKASAW
Atlantic Ocean
CHUMASH
PUEBLO
CHOCTAW
APACHE
COMANCHE
CREEK
NATCHEZ
SEMINOLE

Culture Groups

- Subarctic
- NW Coast
- Plateau
- Great Basin
- California
- Southwest
- Plains
- NE Woodlands
- Southeast
- Others

Gulf of Mexico

0   250 miles
0   500 kms

© Oxford Cartographers

Named on this map are the biggest of the many Native American nations, or tribes, that lived in North America when European exploration and settlement began. Modern scholars have sorted the Indian peoples into ten large cultural groups, each living in a different part of the continent and following its own way of life. English and French settlers first met Indians of the Northeast Woodlands cultural group, who hunted, farmed, and occasionally built large settlements of wooden buildings or joined together in loosely organized states. In the area north of Mexico, Spanish explorers and colonists met members of the Southwest cultural group, skilled at farming in a dry climate and at building **pueblos,** *many-roomed structures of stone or mud-brick.*

and the new leader of the confederacy, declared war on the white settlers with a cunning attack. A colonist later wrote that the Indians "came unarmed into our houses with Deere, Turkies, Fish, Fruits, and other provisions to sell us." The Indians seized the colonists' tools and weapons and killed 350 men, women, and children. The settlers fought back, burning the Indians' houses, stealing their corn, and killing them when they could catch them. In 1644, the Powhatan again attacked the colony. In their counterattack, the colonists captured and killed the aged Opechancanough.

A truce between the Virginia colonists and the Powhatan failed to end the fighting, and a final battle occurred in 1656. This time, some Powhatan warriors sided with the colonists. By the 1670s, the Powhatan were in decline. Some had died in battle, but more fell to smallpox and other diseases that Europeans carried to the Americas.

The Pequot War

The first English colonists in New England received food and advice from Native Americans. Yet many settlers rejoiced that large numbers of Indians had died of European diseases. One Massachusetts colonist called smallpox a sign of "the wondrous wisdom and love of God" because it cleared the land of "Savages."

Among the survivors of the epidemics were

Colonists used both fire and weapons against the Pequot settlement on the Mystic River. Colonist William Bradford wrote, "Those that scaped the fire were slaine with the sword... and very few escaped. It was a fearful sight to see them thus frying in the fyer, and the streams of blood quenching the same...but the victory seemed a sweete sacrifice...."

the wealthy and powerful Pequot, who lived along the Connecticut River. They became enemies of the Massachusetts settlers after they killed a trader named Jonathan Stone in 1634. Stone had been kicked out of the colony as a pirate and a criminal. But he was a white man, and his death was an excuse for more fighting. It began in 1636 with an attack on a Pequot village. In response, the Indians promptly laid

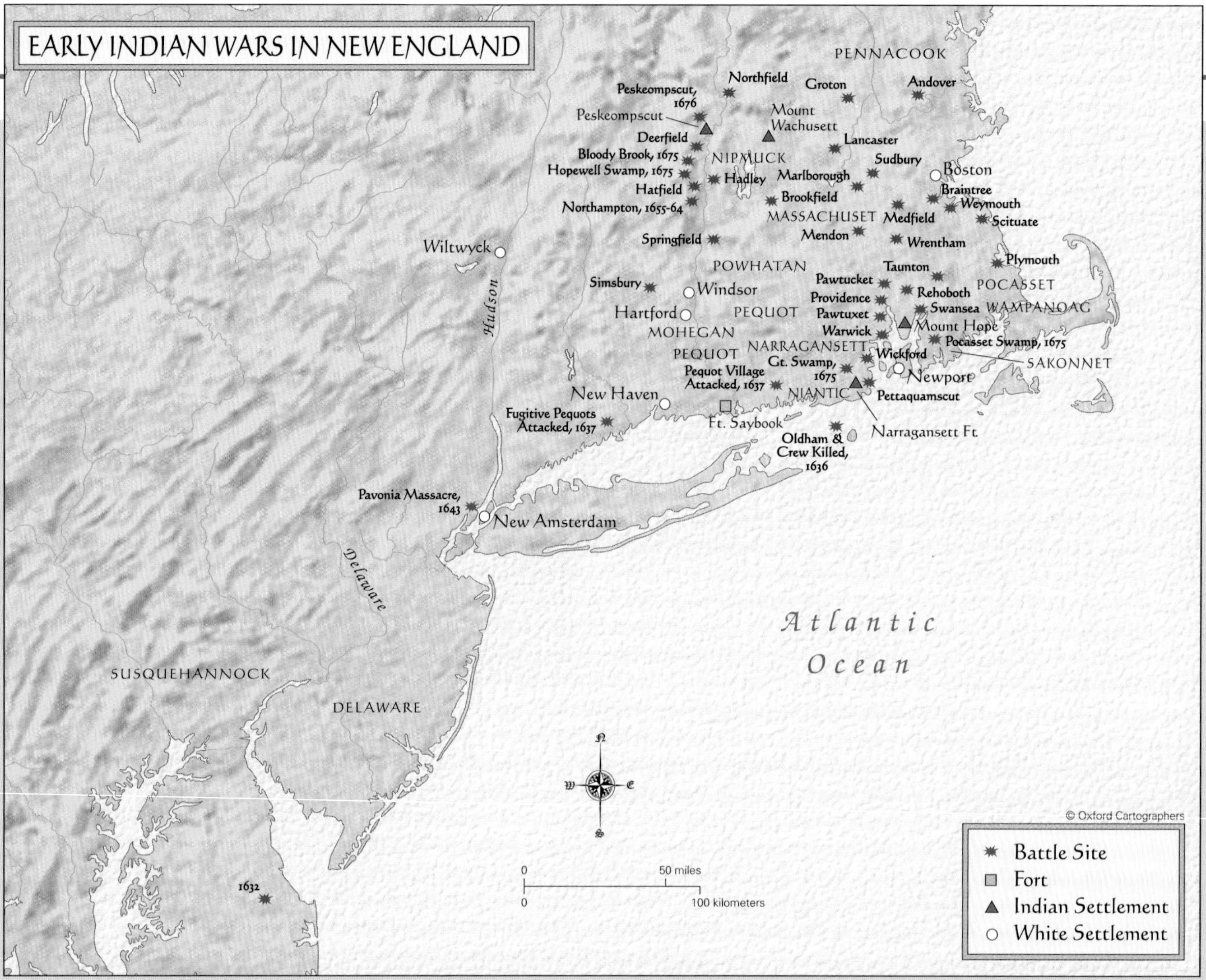

EARLY INDIAN WARS IN NEW ENGLAND
PENNACOOK
Northfield
Groton
Andover
Peskeompscut, 1676
Peskeompscut
Mount Wachusett
Deerfield
Lancaster
Bloody Brook, 1675
NIPMUCK
Sudbury
Boston
Hopewell Swamp, 1675
Hadley
Marlborough
Hatfield
Brookfield
Braintree
Weymouth
Northampton, 1655-64
MASSACHUSET
Medfield
Scituate
Mendon
Springfield
Wrentham
Wiltwyck
POWHATAN
Taunton
Plymouth
Simsbury
Windsor
Pawtucket
Rehoboth
POCASSET
Providence
Hartford
PEQUOT
Pawtuxet
Swansea
WAMPANOAG
MOHEGAN
Warwick
Mount Hope
NARRAGANSETT
Pocasset Swamp, 1675
PEQUOT
Gt. Swamp, 1675
Wickford
SAKONNET
Pequot Village Attacked, 1637
Newport
New Haven
NIANTIC
Pettaquamscut
Fugitive Pequots Attacked, 1637
Ft. Saybook
Oldham & Crew Killed, 1636
Narragansett Ft
Hudson
Pavonia Massacre, 1643
New Amsterdam
Delaware
Atlantic Ocean
SUSQUEHANNOCK
DELAWARE
N
W
E
S
© Oxford Cartographers
0
50 miles
0
100 kilometers
1632
Battle Site
Fort
Indian Settlement
White Settlement

New England's early years were peppered with conflict. At the root of the conflict was the settlers' belief that the Indians had no real right to the land because they did not use it for cities and large-scale agriculture, as the Europeans did. Although some Native Americans did occupy big, long-lasting settlements, many lived in small groups that built temporary shelters and moved often. Their way of life seemed foreign and primitive to Europeans. Many of the white settlers also felt that their Christian religion gave them a claim on the Indians' land. Quoting from the Bible's Psalms—"Ask of me, and I shall give thee, the heathen for thine inheritance, and the uttermost parts of the earth for thy possession"—they argued that God meant for them to rule over the heathen, or non-Christian, Indians and to possess the whole earth.

siege to a colonial outpost called Fort Saybrook. Raids and **skirmishes** continued until large-scale war broke out in 1637. Several hundred colonists, with more than five hundred allies from the Narrangansett and Mohegan tribes, set fire to a Pequot stronghold on the Mystic River. Most of the Pequot warriors were elsewhere, and the attack was a massacre of more than 600 women, children, and old men. By the next year, the colonists had either killed the remaining Pequot or sold them as slaves to rival Indian tribes.

Did the murder of Stone really cause the Pequot War, as the colonists claimed? Probably not. The Massachusetts and Connecticut colonies were competing for control of the Connecticut River Valley, and both wanted the Pequot out of the way. (The colonists may have also hoped that defeating one tribe would frighten other Indians into peaceful behavior.) The Native Americans were drawn into a conflict among the Europeans, and the Europeans took advantage of Indian rivalries, playing tribes against each another and winning **allies** with gifts.

King Philip's War

The Pequot War created bad feeling between the New England colonists and their Native American neighbors, but Massasoit, chief of the Wampanoag, was friendly toward the English. When he died in 1661, his son Wamsutta became chief. The Plymouth and

Rhode Island colonies wanted the Wampanoag lands and began harassing Wamsutta. Arrested and imprisoned in Plymouth, Wamsutta fell ill

Metacom, or Metacomet, was a Wampanoag leader whom the colonists called King Philip. The settlers considered him especially threatening because he tried to unite several separate Indian groups into a larger and more organized force to fight the whites. Other Native American leaders would later have the same dream.

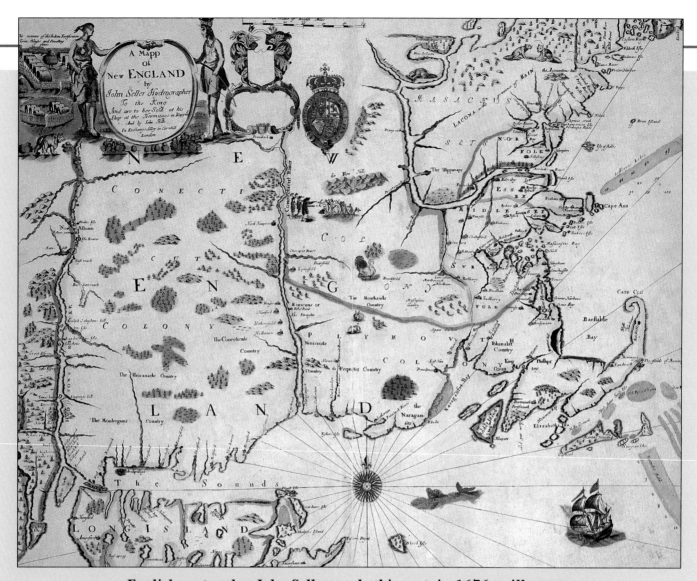

English mapmaker John Seller made this map in 1676 to illustrate King Philip's War, which had just ended in New England. The drawing to the left of the title illustrates "Indian Fortifications" and "Dwelling Places." The conflict sketched in the center of the map, with colonists and Indians firing on each other, may represent a Pequot attack on the village of Hadley in September of 1675. Also scattered across the map are images of animals, including a bear, a wild turkey, and a deer. Mapmakers of this period liked to decorate their maps with drawings, which were usually meant to be educational as well as ornamental.

and died. Leadership fell to his brother Metacom, or Metacomet, whom the colonists called King Philip.

Philip hated being bullied and taxed by the increasingly powerful colonial governments. At the same time, he tried to use the English for his own purposes by turning them against the Narragansett tribe, rivals of the Wampanoag. This plan failed, so Philip made an **alliance** with the Narragansett against the English. War broke out in 1675, with Indian attacks on outlying settlements and villages. The Plymouth, Massachusetts, and Rhode Island colonies set aside their differences to unite against the Indians.

In the conflicts that followed, at least six hundred colonists died violently, and a dozen of their villages were destroyed. But although the Indians spread terror through the region, the colonial forces had more men and better weapons. As the number of dead Indian warriors approached three thousand, Philip's allies abandoned him. In 1676, the colonists captured Philip's wife and son, then the chief himself. They killed Philip and sold his family and surviving followers as slaves.

BEST-SELLING TALES OF CAPTIVITY

 King Philip's War produced one of America's first best-selling books, *The Captivity and Restoration of Mrs. Mary Rowlandson* (1682). It was the true story of a woman taken prisoner in an Indian raid on Lancaster, Massachusetts, in 1676. "Some in our house," she wrote about the raid, "were fighting for their lives, others wallowing in their blood, the house on fire over our heads, and the bloody heathen ready to knock us on the head, if we stirred out." Rowlandson remained a captive for three months before being released in exchange for trade goods.

Stories such as Mary Rowlandson's were very popular. They offered readers both the fright and excitement of a terrifying story and the satisfaction of knowing that the sufferer had been restored to Christian civilization. Another best-selling true tale of Indian captivity was *The Redeemed Captive*. It was written in 1706 by a minister named John Williams, who had been taken prisoner during an Indian raid on Deerfield, Massachusetts, two years earlier. Williams received much publicity. But his daughter, Eunice, caused a scandal among the settlers. Also a captive, Eunice married an Indian man and refused to return to white society. Colonial Americans felt betrayed and insulted by anyone who chose to live among the Indians.

EUROPEAN AND NATIVE SETTLEMENT, EARLY 1700s

European settlements
- British
- French
- Spanish

European influence
- British
- French
- Spanish
- Area of overlapping British & French influence

© Oxford Cartographers

Hudson Bay

HUDSON'S BAY COMPANY

NEW FRANCE

HIDATSA

ABENAKI
Quebec
NOVA SCOTIA

MANDAN
ALGONQUIN
Montreal

Boston

ARIKARA
SIOUX
FOX
Detroit
IROQUOIS
New York
Philadelphia
Atlantic

LOUISIANA
DELAWARE
Ocean

PAWNEE
Cahokia
SHAWNEE
Williamsburg

TUSCARORA

Santa Fe Taos
CADDO
CHICKASAW
CHEROKEE

NAVAJO
Zuni
Pecos
PUEBLOS
COMANCHE
CREEK
CATAWBA
Charleston

ALABAMA
YAMASEE

APACHE
CHOCTAW
NATCHEZ
APALACHEE
St. Augustine

San Antonio
New Orleans

Pacific Ocean

NEW SPAIN

Gulf of Mexico

0   500 miles
0   500 kilometers

By the beginning of the eighteenth century, three European powers were dividing North America among themselves. Spain, France, and Great Britain had settlements along the edges of the continent and were reaching inland. They formed various kinds of relationships with the Native American peoples, from waging war to making alliances. The French reached farther toward the heart of the continent than either of the other two powers, sending traders, missionaries, and settlers along the major rivers that served as inland waterways. By this time, large and long-established Native American settlements, such as Cahokia in the Mississippi River Valley and some of the Pueblo in the Southwest, were surrounded by European activity.

The Pueblo Revolt

The English were not the only Europeans who fought Indian wars. In New Mexico, the northern part of Spain's Mexican colony, Native Americans rebelled against Spanish colonists in the Pueblo Revolt, named for the villages, called *pueblos*, in which the Indians of the Southwest lived.

In 1598, Spanish settlers, soldiers, and priests arrived in New Mexico. They wanted to stamp out the Native American religions by forbidding Indians to practice them. And although Spain had outlawed slavery in its colonies, the Spanish treated Indians much like slaves. The Indians grew angry, and in 1680, after Spanish officials hanged several Indian religious figures, the Pueblo Indians revolted. Their leader was named Popé. He and his warriors destroyed many Spanish settlements and killed more than four hundred people in the colonial capital of Santa Fe. The Spanish survivors fled, and Popé became the new ruler of the region, settling into the governor's palace. After his death in 1688, the fragile alliance among the Pueblo groups fell apart. The Spanish began reconquering the area in 1692, by capturing Santa Fe. Three years later, they stamped out the last of the revolt, and they moved back into Pueblo country.

The French and Indian War

The French and Indian War may seem misnamed. It was not a war between the French and the Indians. In fact, it was the end of a long struggle between the French and the English (called the British after England formed the union of Great Britain in 1707) for control of North America. The war pitted the British and their Native American allies against the French and *their* allies.

Early in the 1600s, the French founded a colony in what is now Canada. They formed alliances with the Algonquian family of Indian tribes, who lived in Maine and eastern Canada and along the Saint Lawrence River. The Iroquoian tribes, in northern New York and around the eastern Great Lakes, had long been enemies of the Algonquians, so they sided with the English, the enemies of the French. For years, the British and French armed their Indian allies and urged them to attack enemy settlements. One such attack took place in 1689, when Iroquois warriors attacked the French settlement of La Chine, near Montreal. They killed more than sixty people and captured nearly one hundred. In 1704, a mixed force of French and Abenaki Indians raided the village of Deerfield, Massachusetts, killing fifty colonists and taking one hundred prisoners. Many similar incidents occurred, and whites and Indians on both sides committed **atrocities**.

When France and Great Britain went to war in 1756, renewed fighting broke out on the colonial frontier. At first, things went well for the French and their allies. In 1759, however,

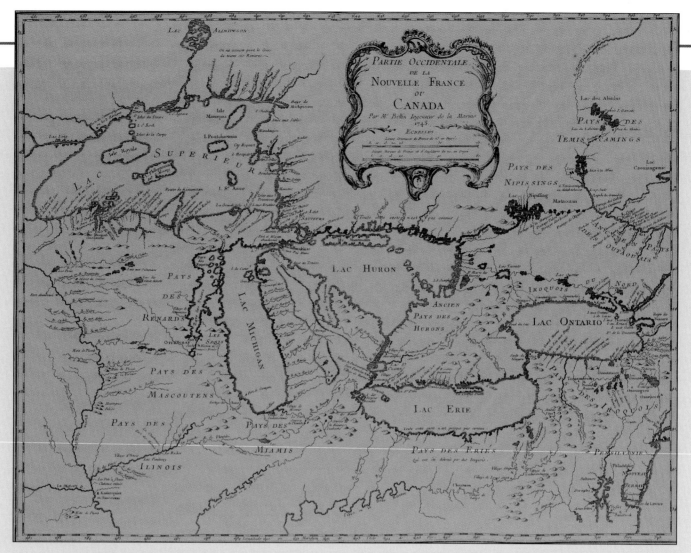

This map of the Great Lakes region appeared in 1744 in a French book about North America. Jacques Nicolas Bellin, one of the finest mapmakers of his day, based the map on maps, sketches, and journal notes by many explorers and travelers. It shows the location of various Indian nations known to the French—"Pays des Iroquois," for example, means "Country of the Iroquois." The map shows waterways in great detail because these were the routes by which Europeans explored the region.

the British captured the French fortress of Quebec, and the fortunes of war shifted.

Pontiac, a chieftain of the Ottawa people, feared a British victory. He knew that the

British sent far more colonists to their territories than the French, and that they were less respectful of Indian culture. In the spring of 1763, Pontiac tried to unite the Great Lakes tribes against the British. Although he captured some forts and killed some settlers, his effort collapsed a few months later when France surrendered its North American territory to the British. The long war between the British and French had ended—but the Indians were not done fighting.

British troops led by General James Wolfe defeat the French defenders of Quebec led by Louis Joseph Montcalm, who lies fatally wounded before Wolfe. The loss of Quebec during the French and Indian War was a major defeat for the French and their Native American allies.

Pontiac was another Native American leader who dreamed of uniting many tribes into a single fighting force to resist white settlement. Although Pontiac's plan led to the attacks on twelve British forts—and the destruction of eight of them—he gave up the battle after France lost the French and Indian War and some Great Lakes tribes made peace with the British. Pontiac finally signed his own peace treaty in 1766. He was murdered three years later by an Indian of the Illinois tribe, an event that led to war between the Ottawa and Illinois peoples.

Chapter Two

THE WARS OF REMOVAL

Perhaps Native Americans and white settlers could never have shared North America in peace. Most conflicts between them arose from differing ideas about land and government. Europeans believed that each piece of land had a definite owner and that every nation had a ruler who could make decisions and sign **treaties** on behalf of all. Such ideas were foreign to the Indians. Tribes often fought over territory, but the winners were not considered permanent owners of the land. And although chieftains could wield great power, Indians did not feel that their leaders had the right to speak or act for everyone. Europeans who got chieftains to sign treaties of land sale regarded themselves as the legal owners of the land, but most Indians would not leave their homelands just because some chieftains had made marks on a piece of paper. All too often, these differences led to violence.

Beyond the Mountains

Many Indians had fought the British during the French and Indian War. But in 1776, when the American colonists began fighting for independence from Britain, most of the Indians in eastern North America sided with the British. They feared the land hunger of the Americans, and rightly suspected that settlers wanted to move into Indian lands west of the Appalachian and Allegheny mountain ranges. After being defeated by Virginia troops in 1774, the Shawnee Indians had already given up territory in Kentucky.

During the Revolutionary War, Britain's Indian allies attacked many colonial settlements. One of the bloodiest battles occurred in Pennsylvania's Wyoming Valley in 1778, when a band of British troops, Indian allies, and Tories (colonists who remained loyal to Britain) ambushed colonial troops and killed three hundred of them, burning some alive and scalping others. Such deeds were sadly common in the Indian wars of the frontier, which continued long after the Revolutionary War ended in 1783.

During the 1780s, Americans pushed westward, over the mountains and into the Ohio River Valley. At that time, what is now Ohio was part of the Northwest Territory, a large region also including the present-day states of Indiana, Illinois, Michigan, Wisconsin, and part of Minnesota. The U.S. government sent troops into the region, partly to control the Indians and partly to keep settlers from squatting on land without paying for it. Native American forces won some impressive victories over army troops, especially in 1791, when a Miami and Shawnee force smashed the army of General Arthur St. Clair, losing only twenty-one warriors in a battle that killed 600 of St. Clair's soldiers. Three years later, however, General Anthony Wayne led U.S. troops to an important victory over the Miami and Shawnee at the Battle of Fallen Timbers in Ohio.

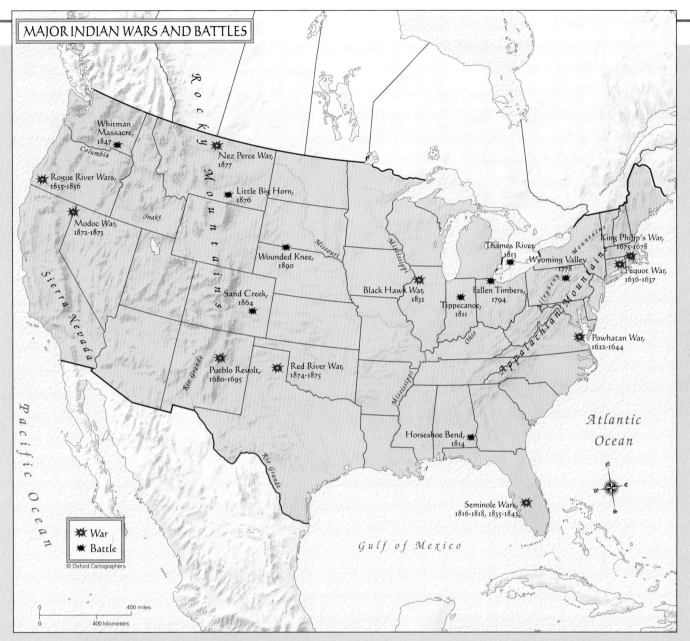

MAJOR INDIAN WARS AND BATTLES

Whitman Massacre, 1847

Nez Perce War, 1877

Rogue River Wars, 1855-1856

Little Big Horn, 1876

Modoc War, 1872-1873

Wounded Knee, 1890

King Philip's War, 1675-1678

Thames River, 1813

Wyoming Valley, 1778

Pequot War, 1636-1637

Black Hawk War, 1832

Fallen Timbers, 1794

Tippecanoe, 1811

Sand Creek, 1864

Powhatan War, 1622-1644

Pueblo Revolt, 1680-1695

Red River War, 1874-1875

Horseshoe Bend, 1814

Seminole Wars, 1816-1818, 1835-1843

Rocky Mountains

Sierra Nevada

Pacific Ocean

Atlantic Ocean

Gulf of Mexico

Columbia

Snake

Missouri

Mississippi

Mississippi

Ohio

Rio Grande

Rio Grande

Allegheny Mountains

Appalachian Mountain

War
Battle

© Oxford Cartographers

400 miles
400 kilometers

The Indian wars in what is now the United States spanned more than two and a half centuries, from the Powhatan War in Virginia in the 1620s to the Battle of Wounded Knee in South Dakota in 1890. They also occurred in all parts of the nation. The clashes and campaigns shown here are only the biggest and best-known conflicts between Indians and the Europeans and Americans who wanted their land. Hundreds of other conflicts took place as well. Although disease killed far more Indians than warfare did, the Native American people did not give up their land without a fight.

Wayne forced chieftains to sign the Treaty of Greenville in 1795, opening much of the Northwest Territory to white settlers.

Tecumseh's Dream

A Shawnee warrior named Tecumseh rejected the Treaty of Greenville and became the leader of an antisettler movement. Tecumseh had fought in Kentucky and at Fallen Timbers. He realized that white Americans would not be satisfied until they had seized Indian land all the way to the Mississippi River—the western boundary of the Shawnee nation. In the early 1800s, he began working on a plan to halt their advance.

Tecumseh saw that if the Native American people were to have even a slim chance of holding their ground, they would have to work together. His goal was to create a grand alliance of tribes from Wisconsin to Alabama. He traveled widely, making speeches that won some chieftains and warriors to his cause. Tecumseh's brother, known as the Prophet, also drew supporters with his religious teachings, which urged Indians to reject white influences and to return to the ways of their ancestors. If they did so, the Prophet promised, the Great Spirit would bring them victory. Unfortunately for the Prophet, Governor William Henry Harrison of the Indiana Territory thrashed his army at the Battle of Tippecanoe in 1811. Afterward, Tecumseh

One of many remarkable Native American leaders during the Indian wars was Tecumseh of the Shawnee people. In this portrait, he wears a European jacket and medal that he had received as gifts—a common practice among Indians of the time. Like others before him, Tecumseh tried and failed to unite the various tribes into a single force that could fight an organized war against the whites. An ally of the British in the War of 1812, Tecumseh was killed by American troops in Canada.

split from his disgraced brother, and many of his warriors left the alliance in disgust.

When the War of 1812 broke out between the United States and Great Britain, Tecumseh and his remaining followers sided with the British forces in Canada. In 1813, the Shawnee leader died fighting U.S. troops in the Battle of the Thames, and the dream of the largest

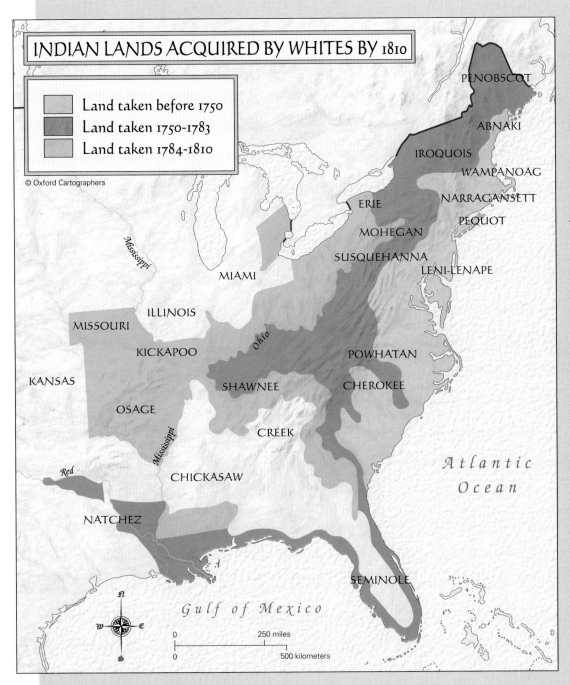

INDIAN LANDS ACQUIRED BY WHITES BY 1810

Land taken before 1750
Land taken 1750-1783
Land taken 1784-1810

© Oxford Cartographers

PENOBSCOT

ABNAKI

IROQUOIS

WAMPANOAG

NARRAGANSETT

ERIE

PEQUOT

MOHEGAN

SUSQUEHANNA

LENI-LENAPE

MIAMI

ILLINOIS

MISSOURI

Ohio

KICKAPOO

POWHATAN

KANSAS

SHAWNEE

CHEROKEE

OSAGE

Mississippi

CREEK

Red

CHICKASAW

Atlantic Ocean

NATCHEZ

SEMINOLE

Gulf of Mexico

0   250 miles

0   500 kilometers

Changes in land ownership in North America followed the path of exploration and settlement. In what is now the United States, the first region explored and settled by Europeans lay along the eastern seacoast. It took about 130 years for whites to acquire most of the land in the original thirteen colonies. After that, the pace of change speeded up. In just thirty-three years, whites claimed the rest of New England, the coastal lands from Florida to the mouth of the Mississippi River, and inland territory reaching all the way to the Ohio River. Then, twenty-six years after the end of the American Revolution, the United States gained control of much of the fertile land in the Ohio and Mississippi River Valleys. As the frontier of white settlement and ownership marched westward, it pushed Native Americans before it, forcing tribes into new territories, where they often came into conflict with the original inhabitants.

TRAPPED AT HORSESHOE BEND

 During the War of 1812, the Creek Indians of the Southeast split into two groups. The White Sticks tried to get along with the whites. The Red Sticks were bent on resistance. In 1813, they attacked a settlement called Fort Mims in Alabama, massacring four hundred people. Enraged settlers in Tennessee sent an officer named Andrew Jackson to end the threat. His large army included some Cherokee and White Stick Creek allies. In early 1814, after wiping out several Red Stick villages, Jackson came upon enemy warriors camped at Horseshoe Bend, a large curve in Alabama's Tallapoosa River. The Creek had camped in the bend because they felt protected by water on three sides. But when Jackson's men began firing on them from the fourth side, the river became a trap. The Indians couldn't retreat. More than 750 warriors died. Their leader, Red Eagle, surrendered to Jackson.

Four years after crushing the Creek warriors at the Battle of Horseshoe Bend in Alabama, Andrew Jackson led troops into Florida, which belonged to Spain. Here, the American invaders prepare to advance on the port of Pensacola, where Spanish ships lie at anchor. Jackson claimed his raids across the Florida border were to chase dangerous Indians, but his true goal was to pressure Spain into giving Florida to the United States. Spain did so in 1819, and Jackson promptly retired from the army and became governor of the new Florida Territory.

This defeat broke the power of the Creek and gave two-thirds of their land in present-day Georgia and Alabama to the whites.

Indian confederacy in North American history died with him. Almost twenty years later, one of Tecumseh's allies, Black Hawk of the Sac and Fox people in Illinois, fought to regain control of his homeland. Black Hawk's revolt, like Tecumseh's, ended in failure.

The Indian Removal Act

In 1758, the British established the first Indian **reservation** in North America as a home for

Thomas Kitchin's map of British territory in North America was published in 1763, at the end of the French and Indian War. The former French colony of New France is now shown as British Canada. The treaty that ended the war also gave Great Britain everything between the Atlantic Coast and the Mississippi River, which is why colonies such as Virginia and the Carolinas appear to stretch westward all the way to the Mississippi. The area along the seacoast is dotted with English place names, while inland the land bears the names of Indian nations, such as "Country of the Cherokees," "Miami," and "Delawares." The British government wanted to leave the inland territory in Indian hands, but it could not stop white settlers from invading the region. A dozen years after this map appeared, the American Revolution began. Its outcome would change the map of North America once again.

about one hundred Indians in New Jersey. After the United States won its independence, it created more reservations, giving various Indian groups parcels of land—although not usually the land they had traditionally inhabited. But some groups, such as the Creek and Cherokee, still held part of their original homelands. After the War of 1812, Americans grew eager to settle these lands. The federal government responded with the Indian Removal Act of 1830, which allowed it to snatch Indian land east of the Mississippi in exchange for land west of the river.

Federal officials claimed that both Indians and whites would be better apart. Eastern Indians would simply be relocated to the Indian Territory on the Great Plains (later limited to present-day Oklahoma). The Indian Removal Act did not authorize force to relocate the Indians, but the federal and state gov-

THE TRAIL OF TEARS

 Among those driven from their homes by the Indian Removal Act were the Cherokee. They resisted abuse and pressure from the state of Georgia, and even won a case in the U.S. Supreme Court, which called Georgia's treatment of the Cherokee unconstitutional. But Andrew Jackson, by then president, refused to enforce the Court's decision. Eventually, the army herded the Cherokee into camps and then, during the bitter winter of 1838–1839, marched them 1,200 miles to the west. A traveler from Maine witnessed the misery of one group of Cherokee: "We found them in the forest camped for the night by the road side...under a severe fall of rain accompanied by heavy wind. With...the cold wet ground for a resting place, after the fatigue of the day, they spent the night...many of the aged Indians were suffering extremely from the fatigue of the journey, and the ill health consequent upon it." Years later, an elderly Cherokee man remembered the journey: "Children cry and many men cry, and all look sad like when friends die, but they say nothing and just put heads down and keep go on towards West. Many days pass and people die very much." The removal involved some 15,000 Cherokee, 4,000 of whom died, either in the camps or on the way west. The Indians called the route the Trail of Tears.

REMOVAL OF EASTERN TRIBES

Lake Superior

Wisconsin Territory

SAUK

FOX

Lake Michigan

Lake Huron

Lake Erie

L. Ontario

MA

VT

NH

NY

MA

CT RI

MI

Mississippi

Missouri

OJIBWAY

OTTAWA

POTAWATOMI

MIAMI

IL

IN

SHAWNEE

OH

PA

MD

NJ

DE

VA

Ohio

MO

KY

NC

Indian Territory

Arkansas Territory

TN

SC

CHICKASAW

CHEROKEE

Red

CHOCTAW

AL

GA

Atlantic Ocean

MS

CREEK

LA

Mississippi

Florida Territory

SEMINOLE

Gulf of Mexico

© Oxford Cartographers

Land ceded to United States by Native Americans

Native American reservations

Cherokee Trail of Tears

Removal routes

0   250 miles
0   500 kilometers

By 1830, when Congress passed the Indian Removal Act, most of the eastern United States no longer had much of a Native Americans population. However, Indians still remained on some large areas—mostly in the South and around the Great Lakes—that were not yet sold or given to the U.S. government. The Act allowed the government to gain control of those remaining Indian lands by moving the Indians to a territory set aside in the West, in what is now Oklahoma. The eastern Indians removed to this territory found themselves in a dry, largely treeless environment that was very different from their homelands. Many found it hard to adapt to life under these new conditions.

ernments applied relentless pressure, denying the Indians their rights and refusing to protect them from squatters and swindlers. In 1831, the Choctaw gave in to this pressure, yielded their land in Alabama and Mississippi, and reluctantly went west. Other tribes followed. One result of the Indian Removal Act was conflict in the West, as the new arrivals jostled the Plains tribes that had long lived in the Indian Territory. Another was the suffering of the eastern Indians, who endured miserable conditions on the long trek.

The Seminole Wars

In 1817, a group of Seminole Indians, a southern branch of the Creek, attacked U.S. troops on the Flint River in Georgia. Although the Seminole were seeking revenge for an army raid on an Indian town, the United States considered their attack an act of war. Before long, Andrew Jackson was again marching to fight Indians. He chased the Seminole into Florida, which then belonged to Spain, and in 1818, he captured a Spanish settlement. His headstrong deed prompted Spain to yield Florida to the United States. (Spain, busy dealing with uprisings in its South American colonies, wanted to avoid war with the United States.) Jackson returned to Tennessee a hero. He had not, however, wiped out the Seminole.

The Indian Removal Act led to the Second

Osceola, the Seminole warrior, as he appeared in 1838. The portrait was painted by George Catlin, a Pennsylvania-born lawyer and artist who dedicated himself to the task of capturing Native American culture and history on canvas.

Seminole War, which began in 1835, when the federal government tried to force the Seminole to move west. Many Seminole refused to be relocated. Under a leader named

Osceola, they put up a fierce fight, attacking white settlers, federal troops, and Indians who accepted the removal plans. The Seminole were masters of ambushes and lightning-fast strikes. Between raids, they hid in Florida's dense, alligator-infested swamps. In 1837, the army captured Osceola through trickery, invit-ing him to a **truce** conference and then imprisoning him. His followers, however, fought on for five more years. After a few thousand Seminole agreed to go west to the Indian Territory, the government stopped chasing those who remained in the swamps of southern Florida's Everglades.

Chapter Three

FIGHTING
FOR THE
WEST

In the early 1800s, Congress gave nearly all the territory between the Missouri River and the Rocky Mountains to the Indians "for as long as the rivers shall run and the grass shall grow." A few years later, Americans began passing through Indian country, bound for Oregon and California. Before long, they wanted to settle the Plains, too—and their desire increased when prospectors found gold and silver in Indian country. In the 1850s, the government started buying back Indian land and moving the Indians onto reservations. The Indians resisted for decades in hundreds of conflicts—all-out wars, raids on isolated camps or settlements, and small but desperate skirmishes. By the 1870s, most chieftains realized that they were doomed to lose the fight. As the sun set over independent Native America, the Indian fighters and Indian warriors of America's last frontier, along with cowboys and sheriffs and gold rushes, became part of the blend of history, legend, and myth that is the Old West.

Bloodshed in the Pacific Northwest

Among the first American settlers in Oregon—which then included present-day Washington State—were missionaries Marcus and Narcissa Whitman. In 1836, they came to what is now Walla Walla, Washington, to offer medical care and Christian teaching to the local Cayuse Indians. The Whitman mission became a regular stop for pioneers on their way west.

In 1847, an **epidemic** of measles broke out around the mission. Most whites recovered from the disease. But measles was fatal to many Cayuse who had never been exposed to it, and some of the Indians suspected that the missionaries were spreading the disease to kill them. A band of warriors attacked the mission, killing a dozen people, including the Whitmans, and taking others captive. White settlers in Oregon

A dramatic image of the Cayuse attack on the home of missionaries Marcus and Narcissa Whitman. White settlers and soldiers were outraged at the attack and vowed revenge on the Cayuse. The Oregon City newspaper declared: "Let [the Indians] be pursued with unrelenting hatred and hostility . . . let them be hunted as beasts of prey; let their name and race be blotted from the face of the earth. . . ."

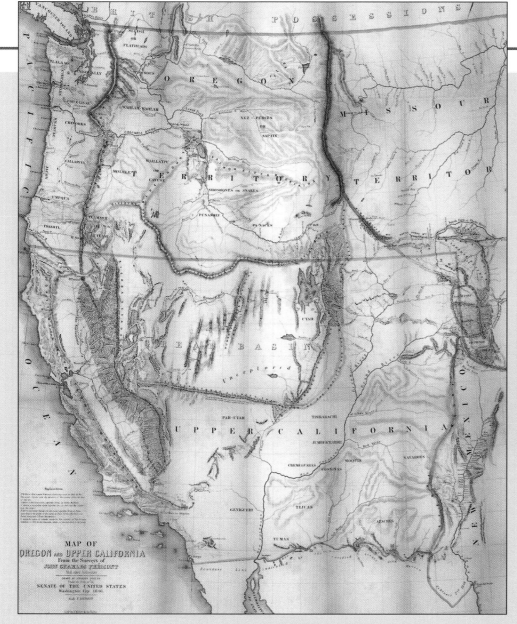

John Charles Frémont, an engineer and explorer for the U.S. Army, published this map of the West in 1845 in a book describing his journeys to the Rocky Mountains and beyond. The areas labelled "Great Basin" and "Upper California" belonged to Mexico. The map shows the few European, Mexican, or American settlements in the West, such as Astoria and Fort Vancouver in the Oregon Territory and San Francisco in California. Most of the West, however, is inhabited only by Native Americans, whose tribal names appear in their various territories. Frémont strongly believed that the West should belong to the United States, and his map was a huge help to the American explorers, prospectors, and settlers who ventured into the region.

responded by making war on many local tribes, not just the Cayuse. Anger on both sides poisoned relations between whites and Indians in the Northwest for years.

In 1855, the Rogue River Wars erupted in southern Oregon. After drunken Rogue Indians killed eleven miners, settlers attacked an Indian camp, murdering not the killers, but rather twenty-three old people, women, and children. The next day, Indian warriors slaugh-

THE UNITED STATES MOVES WEST

■ U.S. Military Forts
○ Cities

CEDED BY BRITAIN

OREGON COUNTRY

LOUISIANA PURCHASE

CEDED BY MEXICO

TEXAS ANNEXATION

GADSDEN PURCHASE

MEXICO

Portland
Ft. Benton
Ft. Berthold
Virginia City
Bozeman
Bozeman Trail
Ft. Boise
Oregon Trail
Snake
Ft. Hall
Ft. Robinson
Ft. Laramie
Oregon Trail
North Platte
Mormon Trail
Nauvoo
California Trail
Great Salt Lake
Ft. Bridger
Sacramento
Central Overland Route
Salt Lake City
South Platte
Ft. Kearny
Sutter's Fort
San Francisco
Old Spanish Trail
Bent's Fort
Ft. Riley
Ft. Leavenworth
Independence
St. Louis
Ohio
Ft. Defiance
Santa Fe
Santa Fe Trail
Cimarron Cutoff
Dodge City
Arkansas
Ft. Gibson
Los Angeles
Colorado
Rio Grande
Ft. Union
Fort Smith-Santa Fe Trail
Ft. Smith
San Diego
Ft. Apache
Ft. Sumner
Ft. Sill
Red
Mission Road
Tucson
El Paso
Ft. Stockton
Butterfield Overland Mail Trail
Rio Grande
Pacific Ocean
Gulf of Mexico
Lake Superior
Lake Michigan
Mississippi
Missouri
Sierra Nevada
Rocky Mountains

0 ———— 400 miles
0 ———— 400 kilometers
© Oxford Cartographers

In the first half of the nineteenth century, the United States expanded to the Pacific Ocean. The first step was the Lousiana Purchase (1803). Fifteen years later, Great Britain ceded, or gave up its claim to, an area along the U.S.-Canada border at the head of the Mississippi. After winning independence from Mexico, Texas joined the United States in 1845, and the next year the United States and Britain agreed on the border between the Oregon Country and Canada. In 1848, after a war with Mexico, the United States took control of California and the Southwest. Five years later, the United States bought the Gadsden Purchase along the Mexican border. Trails snaked across the western territories, and along these trails came traders, missionaries, settlers—and soldiers to deal with the Native Americans who lived in the territories that other nations had bought, sold, or traded away.

tered twenty-seven settlers and burned their town. Raids and attacks by both sides continued for a year, until the army defeated the Rogue warriors and sent the tribe to a reservation. Similar wars occurred in the 1850s near Yakima, Washington, and Coeur d'Alene, Idaho. The Coeur d'Alene War broke out after Indians learned that the U.S. government planned to build a major road through their land without even asking permission, let alone buying the land. It ended in the hanging of the tribe's leaders and the removal of the people to a reservation.

Moving to a reservation was not always the end of the fight, as the Modoc Indians of southern Oregon and northern California learned after surrendering to reservation life in 1864. Starving on the poor land, a few Modoc escaped and returned to their traditional hunting territory in 1872. The army tried to force them back onto the reservation, and the Indians fled to remote lava beds. The rugged landscape was a natural fort, but a poor source of food and water, and the Modoc had to surrender in 1873. Captain Jack, their leader, was hanged, along with some of his men. The rest of the Modoc were sent to a reservation in the Indian Territory.

The Navajo and Apache Wars

For several centuries, Texas, New Mexico, and Arizona belonged to Mexico. When the United States annexed these territories in the mid-1840s, it inherited strife with the Navajo and Apache, who had long battled the Spanish and the Mexicans. When Americans began settling

The Modoc warrior known to whites as Captain Jack led a doomed resistance among the harsh lava beds of northern California. Captain Jack had not wanted to fight the whites, fearing that the result would be the destruction of his people. Other warriors shamed him into it by mockingly placing a woman's basket on his head, which was a way of calling him a coward.

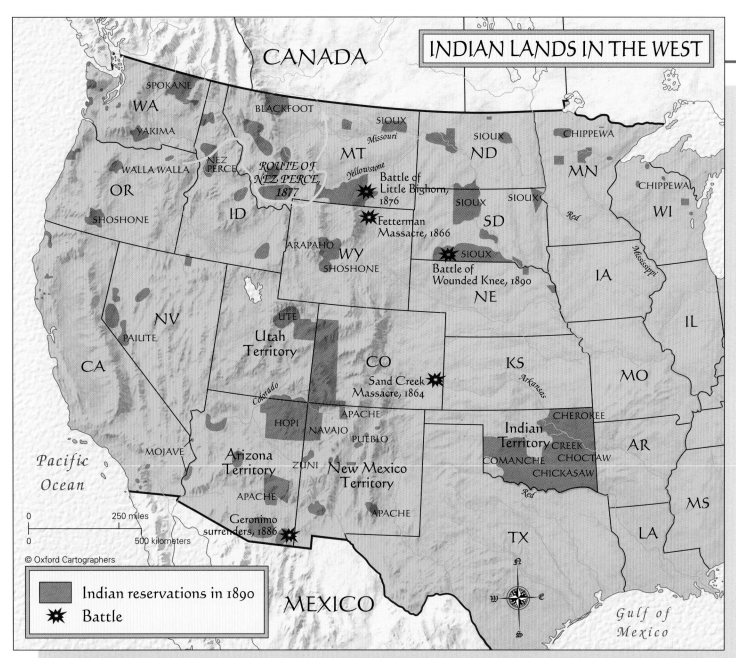

CANADA

SPOKANE

WA

BLACKFOOT

SIOUX

YAKIMA

Missouri

SIOUX

CHIPPEWA

MT

ND

MN

NEZ
PERCE

WALLA WALLA

*ROUTE OF
NEZ PERCE,
1877*

OR

Yellowstone

Battle of
Little Bighorn,
1876

CHIPPEWA

SHOSHONE

ID

Fetterman
Massacre, 1866

SIOUX

SIOUX

Red

WI

ARAPAHO

WY

SD

IA

Mississippi

SHOSHONE

SIOUX

Battle of
Wounded Knee, 1890

NE

IL

UTE

NV

Utah
Territory

PAIUTE

KS

MO

Arkansas

CA

CO

Sand Creek
Massacre, 1864

Colorado

CHEROKEE

HOPI

APACHE

Indian
Territory

AR

NAVAJO

PUEBLO

CREEK

*Pacific
Ocean*

MOJAVE

Arizona
Territory

ZUNI

New Mexico
Territory

COMANCHE

CHOCTAW

CHICKASAW

MS

APACHE

Red

APACHE

LA

Geronimo
surrenders, 1886

TX

0   250 miles

0   500 kilometers

© Oxford Cartographers

MEXICO

*Gulf of
Mexico*

▮ Indian reservations in 1890

✹ Battle

*By 1890, the U.S. government had ended Native American resistance in the West. It has also
succeeded in forcing most Indians onto reservations. The reservations were generally located
on land that white settlers considered least desirable. However, if something happened to
make reservation land more desirable—such as the discovery of gold or, later, of oil—the
government might well strip the Indians of their rights even to reservation land.*

The Apache chieftain Geronimo was photographed in Mexico shortly before his final surrender in 1886. He spent his remaining twenty-three years selling autographed souvenirs and serving as an attraction at public events such as the St. Louis World's Fair of 1904.

the region, the Indians raided their settlements and stole horses and livestock. Settlers were generally no better, often shooting any Indian, even a peaceful one, on sight.

The Navajo and Apache had refused to be Christianized or "tamed." The U.S. government viewed them as serious threats and tried to bring them under control with a series of military expeditions. The Navajo wars raged from the mid-1840s through the mid-1860s. The final blow fell in 1864, when Christopher "Kit" Carson, a well-known trader and scout, led four hundred men against the last major Navajo base, Canyon de Chelly in northern Arizona. The combination of military force, starvation, and harsh winter weather made most of the Navajo surrender. They were held for four years in a crowded and unhealthy reservation on the Pecos River in New Mexico. In 1868, however, they were granted a new reservation on their home territory.

The Apache wars ravaged the Southwest from the 1860s through the 1890s. Committed to maintaining their traditional way of life, the Apache refused to move to a reservation. Their warriors won a reputation for bravery, as well as for cruelty—even settlers and soldiers admitted that no one fought more courageously than Apache war leaders such as Cochise and Geronimo. By the 1880s, the U.S. military was determined to end the "Apache stampede," even if it took "every available man in the whole Army." In 1886, after pursuing the Apache for several years over thousands of miles in the United States and Mexico, the army accepted the exhausted Geronimo's sur-

"CONQUEST BY KINDNESS"

 Ulysses S. Grant, elected U.S. president in 1868, launched a new plan for dealing with the Native Americans. Called "conquest by kindness," the new plan put civilians who were sympathetic to the Native Americans in charge of the federal government's Indian Bureau, which ran the reservations. The military, which viewed all Indians as hostile, still had authority outside the reservations. For a few years, military and civilian officials struggled for control of Indian policy. Then the Apache wars in the Southwest, together with the 1873 murder of a popular general by the Modoc leader Captain Jack, turned public opinion against the Native Americans. The harsh military approach to Indian policy was back in favor.

render. With the most powerful chieftain no longer in the field, the Apache wars ended within a few years.

The Fate of the Plains Indians

Many western Indians had horses, descendants of animals introduced by the Spanish conquistadores centuries earlier. None were better riders than the Plains tribes, whose warriors could kill with bows or rifles while riding at full gallop.

The Plains Indians endured much as a result of American expansion westward. New tribes migrated into their region after being relocated from the east. Miners and settlers, often acting illegally, occupied Indian land. Hunters slaughtered the herds of buffalo that were the livelihood of the Plains tribes. As early as the 1850s,

Frederic Remington, an American artist known for his images of the West, painted **Custer's Last Charge** *to commemorate the Battle of Little Bighorn. Although the painting shows Custer and his men killing Indians, in reality the Indians killed Custer and his entire force. Little Bighorn was considered one of the worst defeats the U.S. Army had ever suffered.*

A CENTURY OF DISHONOR

Some Americans were ashamed of the way their government treated the Indians—especially after most of the frontier areas were settled and the worst of the Indian wars were over. In 1881, a writer and social activist named Helen Hunt Jackson published *A Century of Dishonor*, a bitter account of U.S. betrayals and atrocities in the treatment of the Native Americans of the West. Jackson also exposed flaws in the reservation system. Many readers were moved to sympathy by Jackson's best-selling novel *Ramona* (1884), a heart-rending tale of the mistreatment of Indians in California.

various Plains groups began resisting the white advance, sometimes massacring settlers. Even though some of the Sioux agreed to live on a South Dakota reservation, the trouble did not stop. Following the discovery of gold in the Black Hills in 1874, miners swarmed across the region, and fights broke out. To restore control, the army tried to force *all* the Sioux onto the reservation. Leaders such as Crazy Horse and

Sitting Bull resisted. The most famous clash between Plains warriors and army soldiers took place in 1876, at the Little Bighorn River in Montana, where a force of Sioux and Cheyenne killed Lieutenant Colonel George Armstrong Custer's army to the last man. Within a few years, however, most of the northern Plains Indians had either been caught or surrendered and were living on reservations.

Farther south, Plains tribes such as the Kiowa, Cheyenne, and Comanche also resisted settlers. Their anger was fueled by the massacre of a peaceful Cheyenne village at Sand Creek, Colorado, in 1864. The conflict on the southern Plains reached its climax in the Red River War of 1874–1875, fought mostly in Kansas and northern Texas. The war ended in the surrender of dozens of chiefs and war leaders, including the Kiowa chief Satanta, so sorrowful over his people's fate that he committed suicide in prison.

The End of Resistance

By the 1880s, the Indian wars were over or drawing to a close. The Nez Percés of the Northwest, led by Chief Joseph, had gallantly fought to keep their Oregon homeland and to stay out of the reservation system, but the army had broken them in 1877. The Utes of Colorado and Utah had resisted the whites until 1879, when Ouray, one of their leaders, saved them from the army's wrath by ending

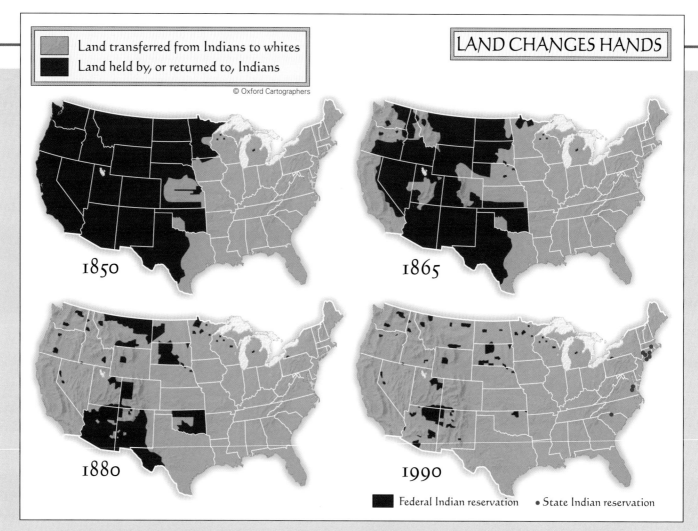

Land transferred from Indians to whites

Land held by, or returned to, Indians

© Oxford Cartographers

1850

1865

1880

1990

Federal Indian reservation   • State Indian reservation

Like the eastern United States, the West steadily passed out of the control of its original inhabitants, the Native Americans. Although Indians controlled the western half of the nation in 1850, by 1880 their territories had shrunk dramatically. A century later, Native Americans held tribal claims to only those lands that had been granted or returned to them in the form of state reservations in the East and federal reservations in the West. The largest reservation today is that of the Navajo people in the Four Corners district, where the borders of Colorado, New Mexico, Arizona, and Utah meet.

the fighting. Even Sitting Bull lived on a North Dakota reservation.

Then, in 1890, the Ghost Dance movement arose among the reservation Sioux. Similar to many other movements in other tribes, Ghost Dance was a revival of traditional Native American religion. It was led by a prophet named Wovoka. He preached that if Indians came together to dance, pray, and perform old rituals, and if they turned away from white goods and customs, the world would change. The buffalo, dead kinsfolk, and the vanished Indian way of life would all return. Wovoka's message brought hope to the despairing Indians, but the rituals and their excitement terrified white settlers and soldiers, who feared an uprising. Trying to head off trouble by arresting Sitting Bull, reservation police—who were Indians—killed the famed chief in a scuffle. A few days later, at Wounded Knee Creek, on a nearby reservation in what is now South Dakota, soldiers came upon a band of Sioux. The soldiers ordered them all to give up their firearms. Though no one knows exactly what happened, the army opened fire, killing about three hundred people—mostly women, children, and elderly people.

The tragedy at Wounded Knee is sometimes seen as the Indians' final defeat. In reality, however, disease and loss of land did more harm to the American Indians than all the atrocities and battles from the time of Columbus to that of Custer. An equally important reality is that although the Indian wars died out by 1890, the Indians did not. Many survived to endure the U.S. government's next policy, assimilation, which was designed to merge Native Americans into mainstream society by doing away with their languages and ways of life. In this new war of culture, the Indians lost much—but, once again, they survived.

Glossary

ally: member of an alliance.

alliance: relationship in which two parties agree to defend each other from their enemies.

atrocity: an especially cruel or brutal act toward an enemy, such as torturing captives or mutilating the dead.

colonist: someone who settles outside his or her country to help bring new territory under control of the home country.

colony: a territory outside the borders of a state but claimed or controlled by that state.

epidemic: an outbreak of disease over a wide area, affecting many people.

missionary: someone who works to convert other people to his or her religion.

reservation: area assigned to Native Americans by the U.S. government.

siege: military operation in which troops surround an enemy fort or city, preventing those inside from escaping or receiving supplies.

skirmish: brief conflict between small groups of combatants.

treaty: formal agreement between peoples or nations.

truce: agreement to stop fighting.

Map List

ABOUT THE HISTORICAL MAPS

The historical maps used in this book are primary source documents found in the Library of Congress Map Division. You will find these maps on pages: 9, 14, 18, 27, and 35.

Chronology

1622–1656	Native Americans and Virginia colonists clash in the Powhatan War.
1636–1637	The Pequot War pits colonists and their Indian allies against the Pequot Indians in New England.
1675–1676	New England colonists fight the Wampanoags and other groups in King Philip's War, named for a Wampanoag leader.
1680–1695	Native Americans in New Mexico rise against Spanish settlements in the Pueblo Revolt.
1794	The U.S. Army defeats Native American forces at the Battle of Fallen Timbers in Ohio.
1814	Andrew Jackson leads militiamen to victory over the Creek Indians at the Battle of Horseshoe Bend in Alabama.
1817–1818	Florida Indians wage the First Seminole War.
1830	U.S. Congress passes the Indian Removal Act, authorizing the relocation of Indians to reservations.
1832	Black Hawk leads the last Native American resistance in the Northwest Territory.
1835–1842	The Seminole are nearly wiped out in the Second Seminole War.
1838–1839	Forced to give up their lands in the Southeast, the Cherokee take the "Trail of Tears" to the Indian Territory in Oklahoma.
1847	A massacre at the Whitman mission launches the Cayuse War in the Oregon Territory.
1860s	The Apache wars of Texas and the Southwest begin.
1872–1873	Rebellious Modoc Indians hide in northeastern California until the army captures their leaders.
1876	Sioux warriors destroy George Armstrong Custer's army at the Battle of Little Bighorn in Montana.
1877	Chief Joseph of the Nez Percé surrenders to the army.
1886	Apache resistance ends when leader Geronimo surrenders.
1890	Sitting Bull is killed. Sioux resistance ends at Wounded Knee Creek, South Dakota.

Further Reading

Axelrod, Alan. *Chronicle of the Indian Wars: From Colonial Times to Wounded Knee.* New York: Prentice Hall General Reference, 1993.

Brown, Dee Alexander. *Bury My Heart at Wounded Knee: An Indian History of the West.* New York: Henry Holt, 2001. (New edition.)

Collier, Christopher and James Lincoln Collier. *The French and Indian War: 1660–1763.* Tarrytown, NY: Benchmark Books, 1998.

Halliburton, Warren. *The Tragedy of Little Bighorn.* New York: Franklin Watts, 1989.

Keenan, Jerry. *Encyclopedia of American Indian Wars, 1492–1890.* New York: Norton, 1999.

Lassieur, Allison. *Before the Storm: American Indians before the Europeans.* New York: Facts On File, 1998.

Nardo, Don, editor. *North American Indian Wars.* San Diego: Greenhaven Press, 1999.

Sherman, Josepha. *The First Americans: Spirit of the Land and the People.* New York: Smithmark, 1996.

Stefoff, Rebecca. *Tecumseh and the Shawnee Confederation.* New York: Facts On File, 1998.

WEBSITES

www.pbs.org/weta/thewest
New Perspectives on the West, based on the eight-part public television series "The West."

www.americanwest.com
Information on Native Americans and U.S. westward expansion; links to dozens of other pages.

www.indianwars.org
Home page of the National Indian Wars Association.

www.users.anderson.edu/~roebuck/war.html
Links to pages about Indian wars in the Northwest Territory (the Ohio River Valley and upper Midwest).

www.kwanah.com/vl/005.htm
Texas Military Forces Museum page on Indian wars. 1800–1860.

ABOUT THE AUTHOR

Rebecca Stefoff is the author of Marshall Cavendish's North American Historical Atlases series and many other nonfiction books for children and young adults. She has written a number of books about the settling of the West, including American Indian history. Stefoff also wrote about the life of one of the most significant Native American leaders in *Tecumseh and the Shawnee Confederation.* She now makes her home in Portland, Oregon.

Index